Stella J. Green
Adult Coloring Book

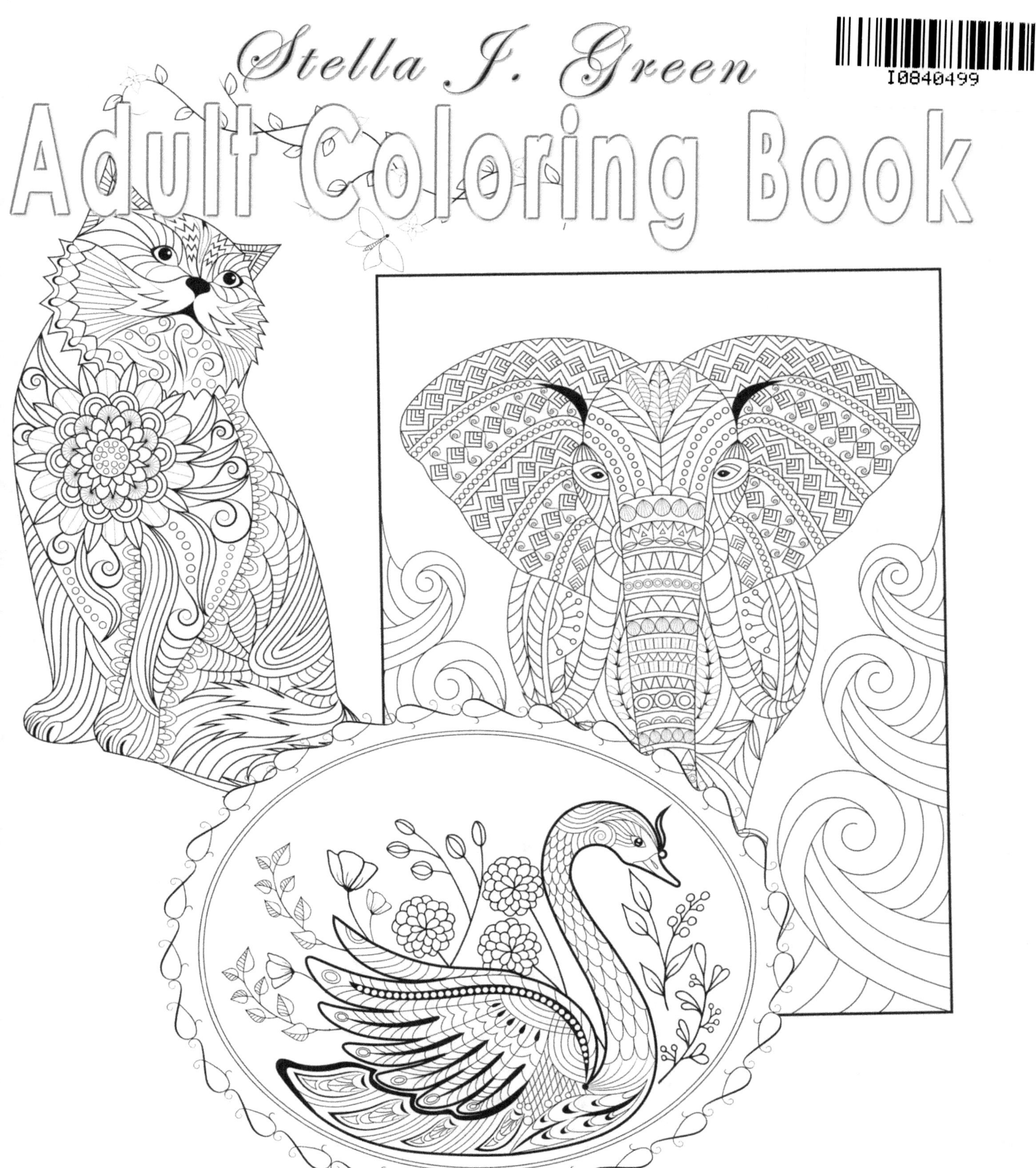

Animal Designs Stress Relieving Illustrations, with Mandala and Paisley Patterns for Relaxation, Mindfulness and Joyful Pastime

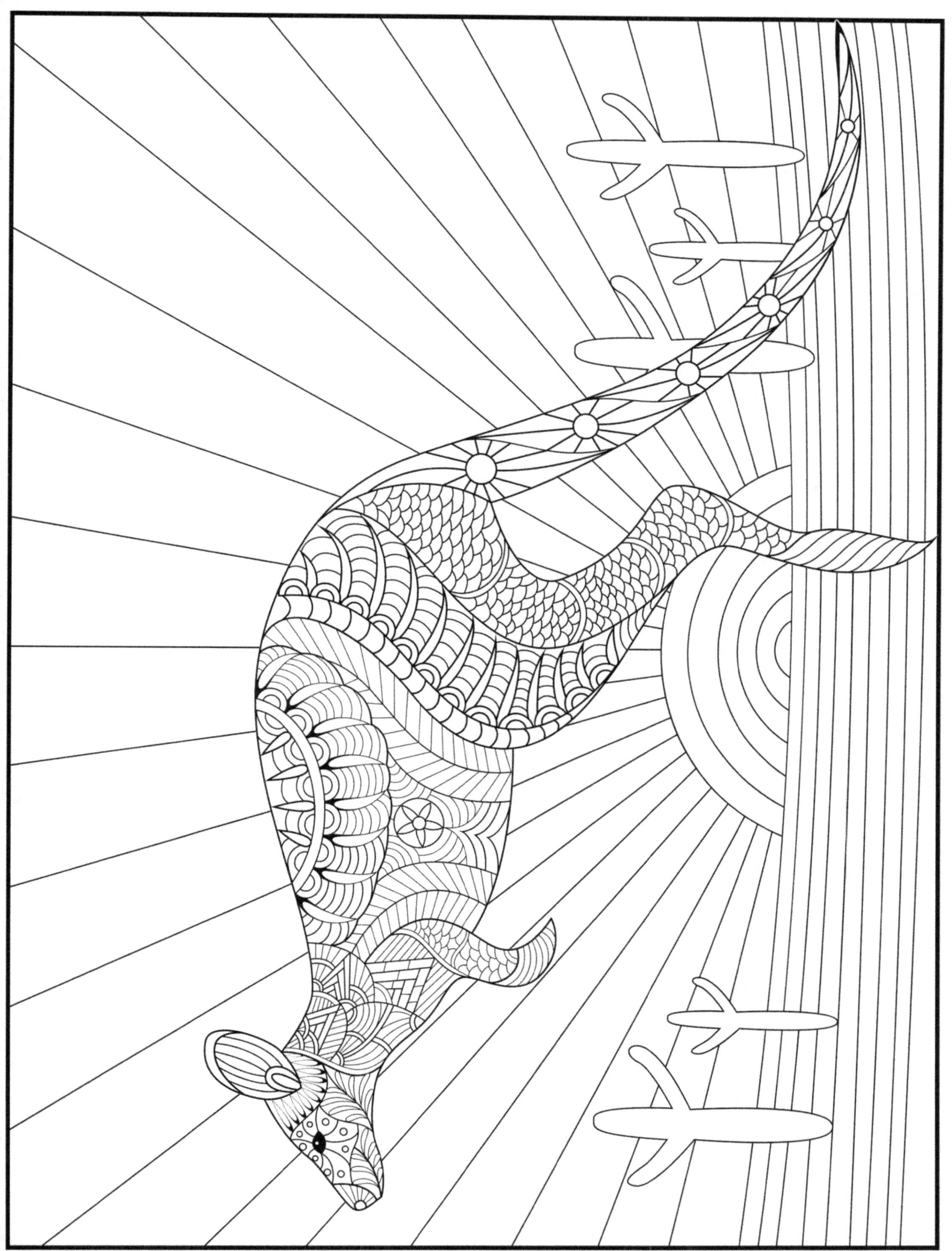

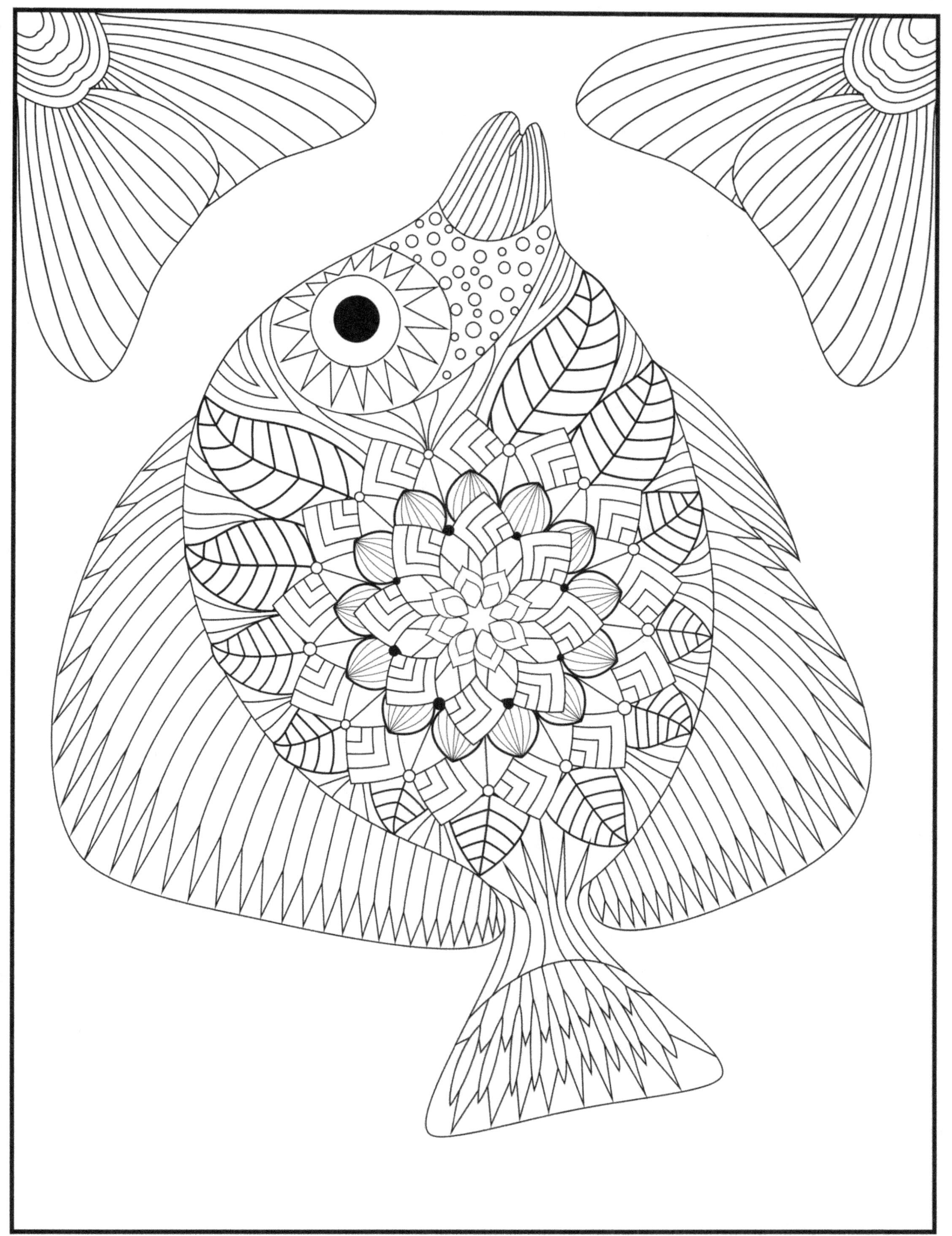

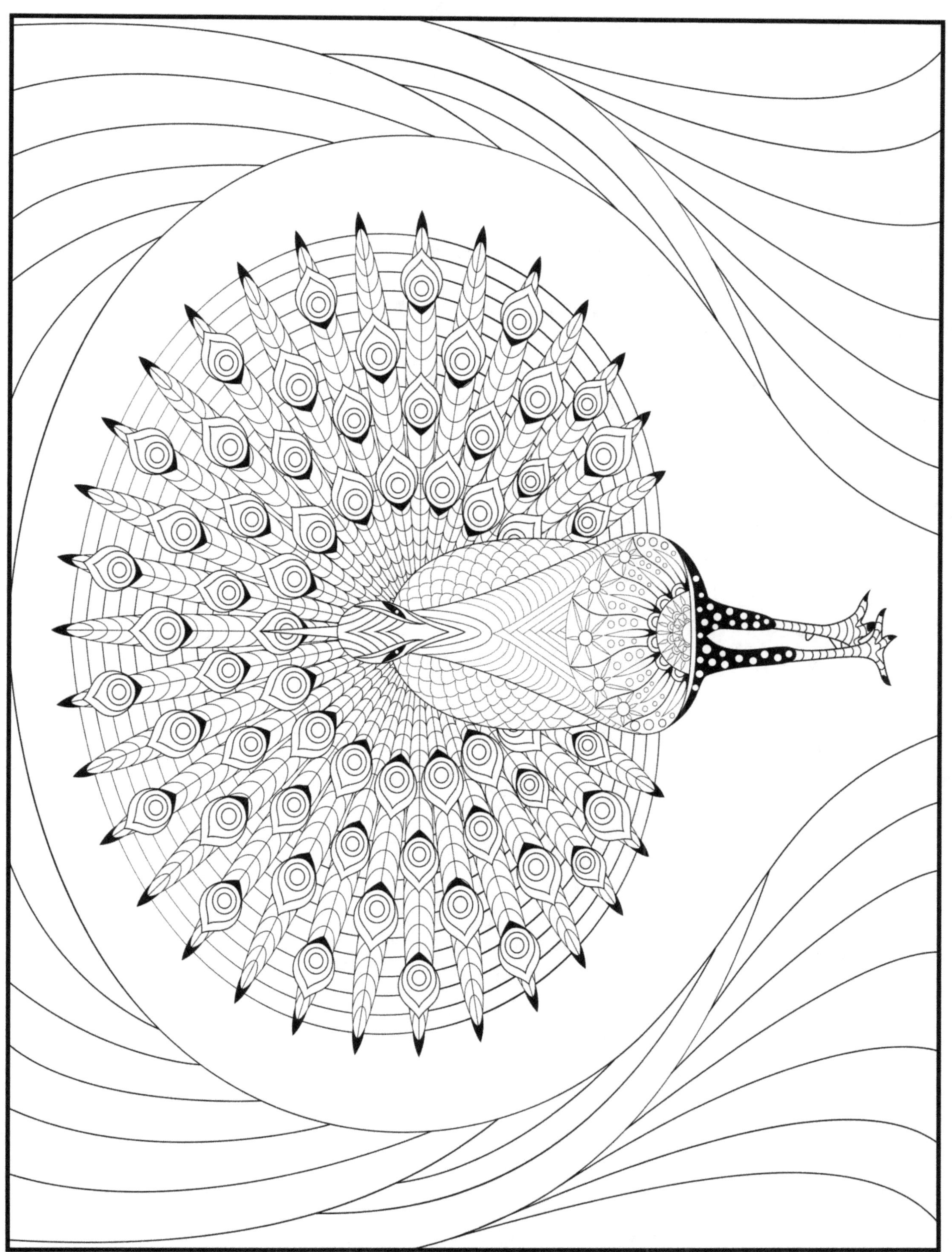

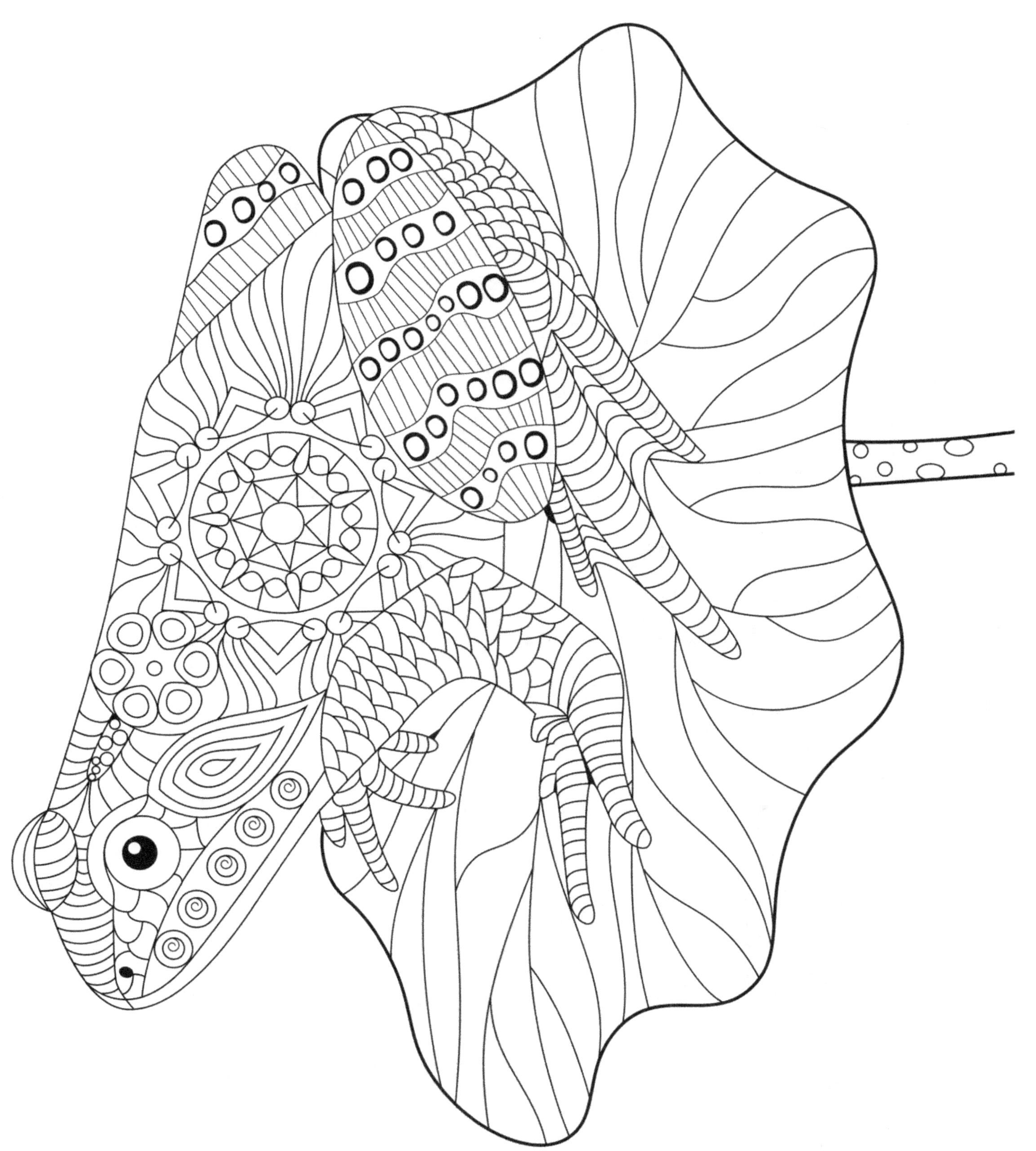

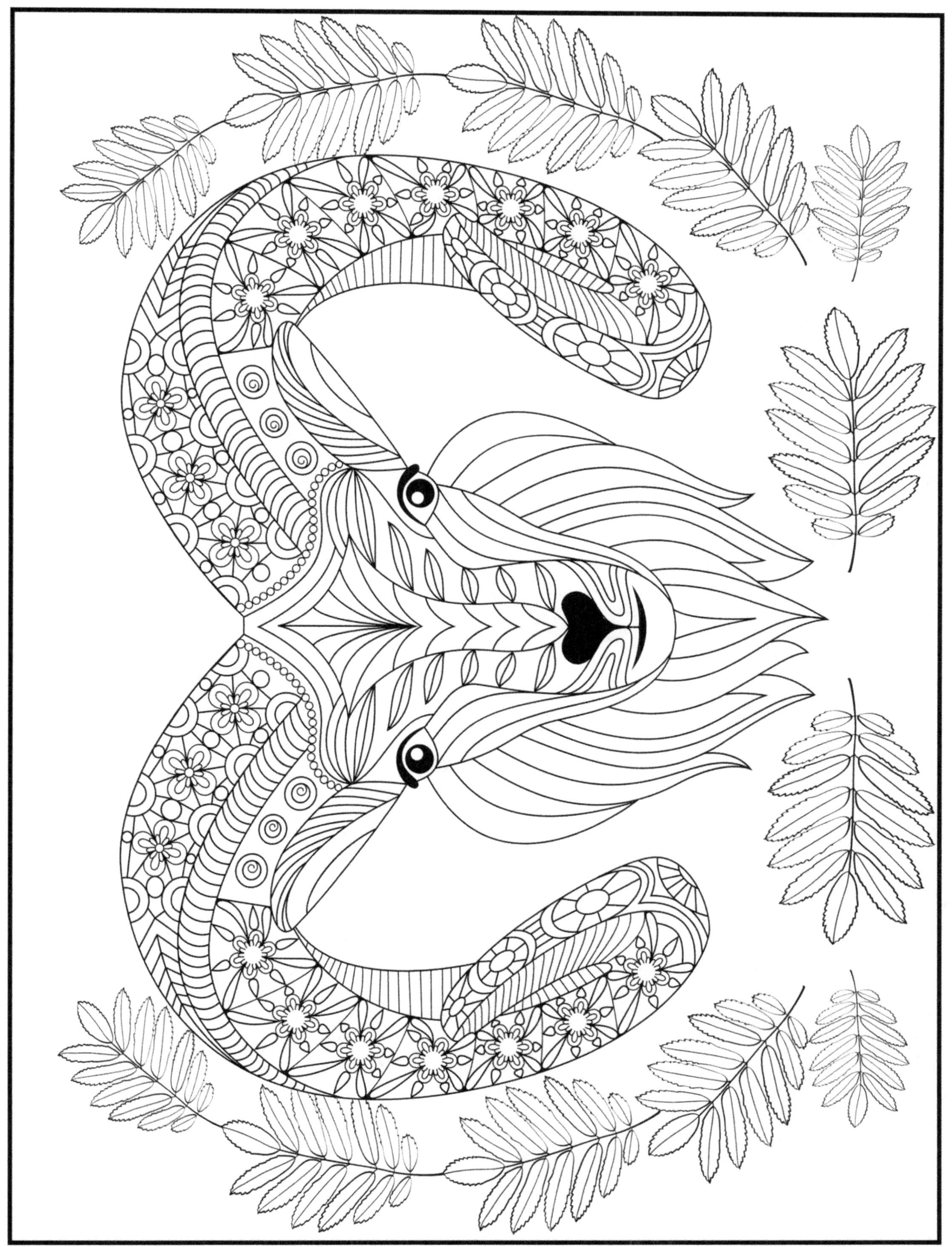

Adult Coloring Book

Animal Designs Stress Relieving Illustrations, with Mandala and Paisley Patterns for Relaxation, Mindfulness and Joyful Pastime

In this inspiring adult coloring book, I have included several original and delightful illustrations of animals featuring beautiful patterns which will allow you to fill pages with your favorite colors to motivate your imagination and inspire your inner-artist. Each drawing invites you to experiment and play with colors, letting them relax your mind and relieve your stress. If you like this book, please take a moment to post a review on www.amazon.com

Enjoy.

Stella Green

About Stella Green

Artist Stella Green loves colors and she studies their influence on people's mood, health and relaxation. She has a degree in Graphic Design, a diploma in Art History and specialized in working with children using art and color therapy.

Adult Coloring Book: Animal Designs Stress Relieving Illustrations, with Mandala and Paisley Patterns for Relaxation, Mindfulness and Joyful Pastime

ISBN: 9781695917767